First Grade Student Notebook
Table of Contents

Lesson
Page

STEMscopes™

CA-NGSS 3D

Student Notebook – First Grade
ISBN: 978-1-63037-594-2

Published by Accelerate Learning Inc., 5177 Richmond Ave, Suite 1025, Houston, TX 77056. Copyright © 2018, by Accelerate Learning Inc. All rights reserved. No part of this publication may be reproduced or distributed in any form or by any means, or stored in a database or retrieval system, without prior written consent of Accelerate Learning Inc., including, but not limited to, in any network or other electronic storage or transmission, or broadcast for distance learning.

To learn more, visit us at www.stemscopes.com

10 9 8 7 6 5 4 3 2 1

This Student Notebook is designed to be used as a companion piece to our online curriculum.

The pages of this book are organized and follow the 5E model.

ENGAGE

Student Handout
A short activity to grab students' interest

EXPLORE

Do
Hands-on tasks, including scientific investigations, engineering solutions, and problem-based learning (PBL)

Claim, Evidence, Reasoning (CER)
A formative assessment in which students write a scientific explanation to show their understanding

EXPLAIN

Linking Literacy
Strategies to help students comprehend difficult informational text

ELABORATE

Reading Science
A reading passage about the concept that includes comprehension questions

EVALUATE

Claim, Evidence, Reasoning (CER)
A summative assessment in which students write a scientific explanation to show their understanding

Open-Ended Response (OER)
A short answer and essay assessment to evaluate mastery of the concept

Only student pages are included in this book and directions on how to use these pages are found in our online curriculum. Use the URL address and password provided to you by your district to access our full curriculum.

Name: _____ Date: _____

 # California Instructional Segment

Take Action!

Design a plant family using the shapes below.
- Draw two parents.
- Draw one offspring based on the two parents.

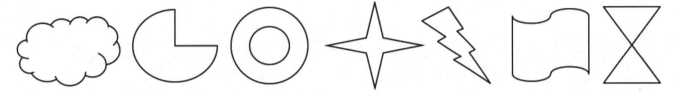

Draw what the family will look like.

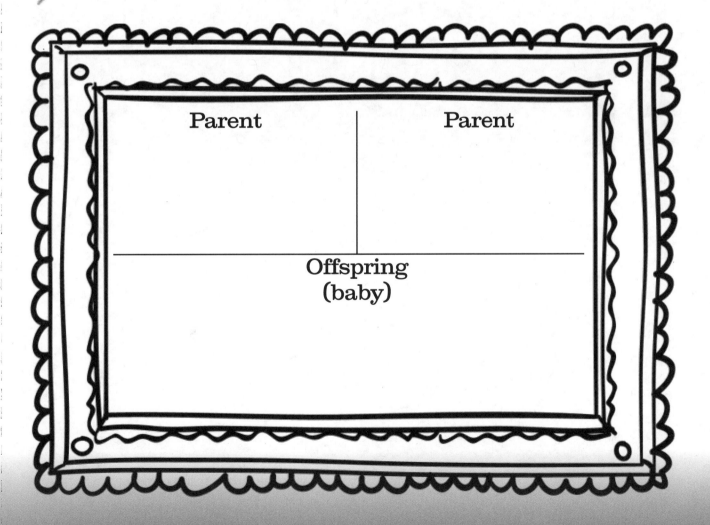

Parent   Parent

Offspring
(baby)

Name: _____ Date: _____

California Instructional Segment

Our Mission:

Plant Family

California Instructional Segment

You and your friends want to play a game after school.

KRAZY
KIDZ
TV

FAMILY

The show will be a cartoon about the plant family's life.

California Instructional Segment

Your job is to design what each plant in the family will look like.

The plants can be drawn using all kinds of shapes and colors.

Be creative!

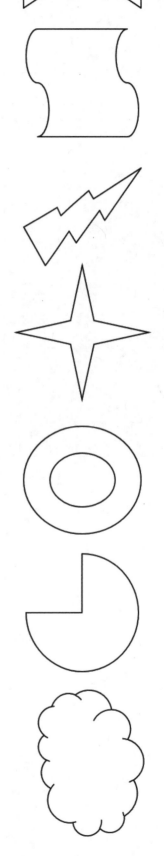

Parts of Plants

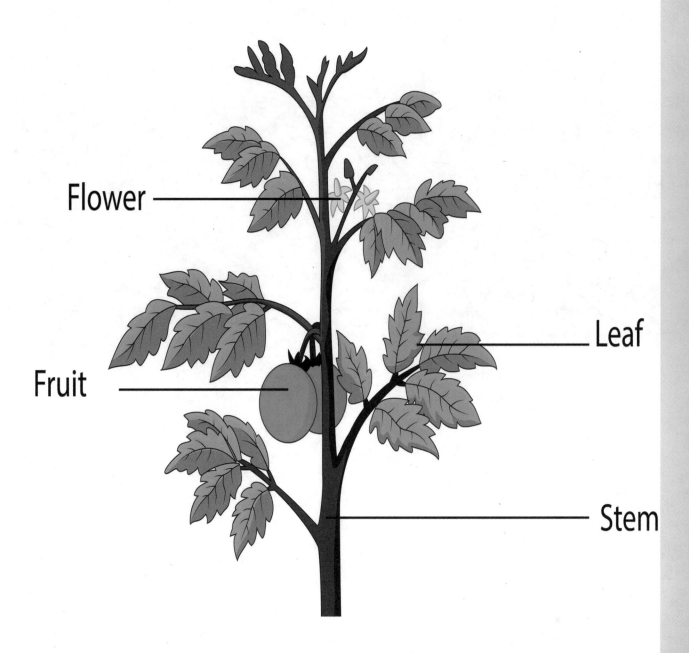

Flower

Fruit

Leaf

Stem

Name: _____ Date: _____

Graphic Organizer

Busy Plants

Directions

Each part of a plant has a job. In the table below, fill in the job that each plant part performs.

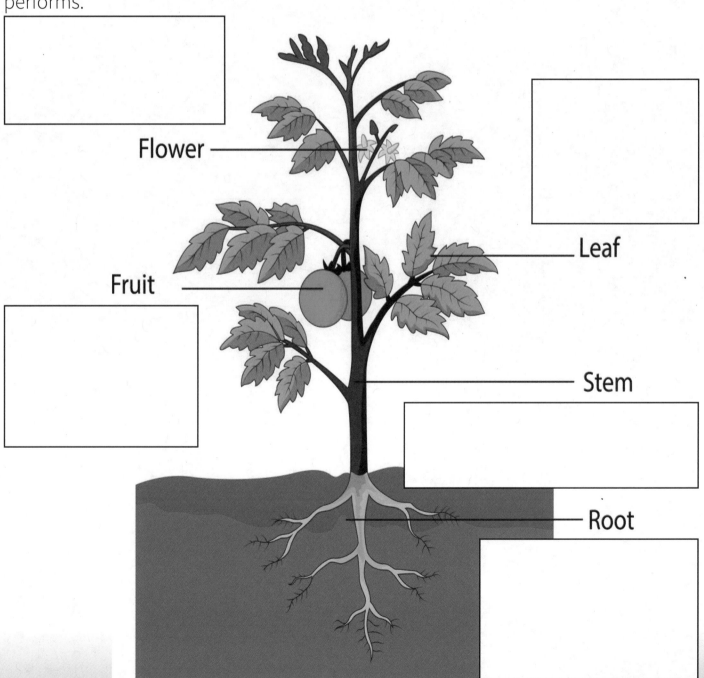

Flower

Leaf

Fruit

Stem

Root

Name: _____ Date: _____

🪝 Hook

Dinnertime!

Label the different parts of a carrot.

_____

- - - - - - - - - - - - - - - - - - - -

_____

_____

- - - - - - - - - - - - - - - - - - - -

_____

_____

- - - - - - - - - - - - - - - - - - - -

Draw and label **a different plant** that you observed today.

Name: _____ Date: _____

 **Explore 1**

Watch It Grow!

Part I

Place a check mark next to each part of a plant you observe.

☐ Roots   ☐ Flower
☐ Stem   ☐ Fruit
☐ Leaves   ☐ Seeds

Part II

Draw and label the plant on your table. Use the word bank to help you spell parts of a plant correctly.

Word Bank
Roots
Stems
Leaves
Flowers
Seeds
Fruit

Explore 1

Part III

Roots

Draw a picture of your lima bean's roots. Then fill in the blank in the sentence.

Plants need roots to...

_____

_ _ _ _ _ _ _ _ _ _ _ _ _ _ _ _ _ _ _

_____

_ _ _ _ _ _ _ _ _ _ _ _ _ _ _ _ _ _ _

_____

_ _ _ _ _ _ _ _ _ _ _ _ _ _ _ _ _ _ _

Stems

Draw a picture of a lima bean's flowers. Then fill in the blank in the sentence.

Plants need stems to...

_____

_ _ _ _ _ _ _ _ _ _ _ _ _ _ _ _ _ _ _

_____

_____

_ _ _ _ _ _ _ _ _ _ _ _ _ _ _ _ _ _ _

_____

_ _ _ _ _ _ _ _ _ _ _ _ _ _ _ _ _ _ _

# Explore 1

Leaves

Draw a picture of your lima bean's leaves. Then fill in the blank in the sentence.

Plants need leaves to...

_____

_____

_____

Flowers

Draw a picture of a lima bean's flowers. Then fill in the blank in the sentence.

Plants need flowers to...

_____

_____

_____

🔍 Explore 1

Fruit

Draw a picture of an apple slice. Then fill in the blank in the sentence.

Plants need fruit to...

_____

_____

_____

_____

Seeds

Draw a picture of your open lima bean. Then fill in the blank in the sentence.

Plants need seeds to...

_____

_____

_____

_____

Name: _____ Date: _____

Explore 2

Humans Mimicking Plants

Which invention that has been inspired by a plant is most useful to you?
Why?

_____

- -

_____
_____

- -

_____

Draw a picture of the plant invention.

Name: _____ Date: _____

 **Explore 2**

Humans Mimicking Plants

Claim Evidence Reasoning

Think about the parts of a plant and their uses. How is this information helpful to humans?

Claim

Write a sentence that answers the question.

_____

- -

_____

_____

- -

_____

Evidence

_____

- -

_____

_____

- -

_____

Explore 2

List examples of the sentence you wrote above.

Draw how you know!

Student Rubric

	3	2	1
Claim	My claim was correct	I made a claim, but it was incorrect	I did not make a claim
Evidence	I gave evidence that helped me make my claim	I gave evidence, but it did not have anything to do with my claim	i did not give any evidence.

Name: _____ Date: _____

 **Explore 3**

Helpful Parts

Draw how you think you will solve the problem.

What will you need to solve the problem? Draw or list the materials here.

Did your solution work? (yes or no)

Use the box below to draw how you could make your solution better.

If you have time, make changes to your solution to make it better.

Name: _____ Date: _____

 # Linking Literacy

Fill in the Diagram

WHILE you read:

Fill in the blanks at the bottom with the parts of the plant as they are described in the STEMscopedia. Cut the boxes on the dotted lines and place them on the correct part of the diagram.

The _____
- anchor the plant in soil and
- soak up water and nutrients.

The _____
- use water, sunlight, and air to make food.

The _____
- can have colorful petals and seeds;
- the seeds grow into new plants.

The _____
- brings things up and down and
- moves food and water to the rest of the plant.

Name: _____ Date: _____

Linking Literacy

Parts of Plants: Three-Column Chart

Part of the Plant	Illustration	Function (how it helps the plant)

Name: _____ Date: _____

Reading Science

The Parts of a Plant

Reading Science

First Grade: Parts of Plants

 **Reading Science**

There are many different kinds of plants.
Do you know all the parts of a plant and
how the parts help it stay alive?

This is a pumpkin plant.
Can you name the parts?

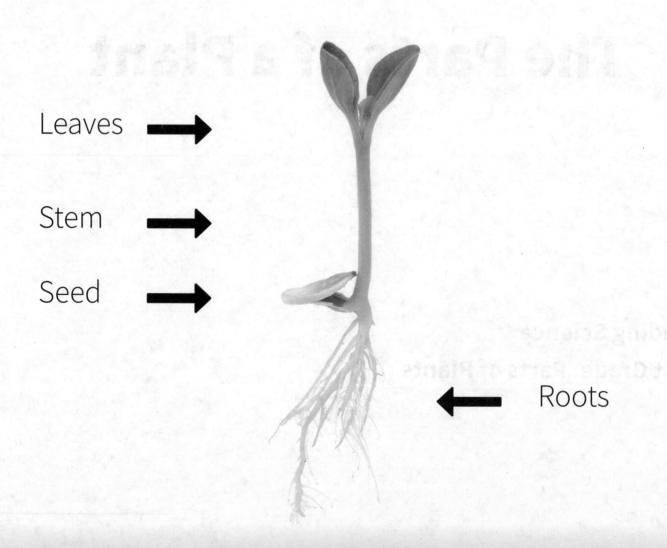

Leaves →

Stem →

Seed →

← Roots

Before it grows, the seed holds the plant.

Seed ➡️

The roots bring water and food
from the soil and into the plant.

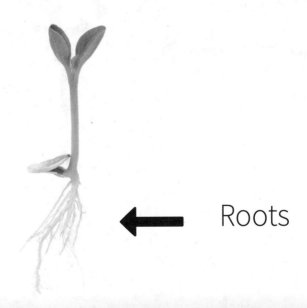 ⬅️ Roots

The stem carries water to the leaves and supports the plant.

Stem ➡️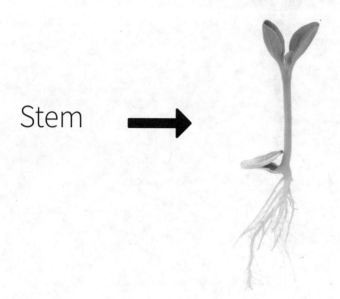

The leaves catch light from the Sun.
The plant uses the Sun's energy to make food.

Leaves ➡️

Reading Science

The pumpkin plant will soon make a flower.

Do you see the baby pumpkin?

The flower's job is to make the seeds.

This is the fruit of the pumpkin plant.

If you break open the pumpkin, what will you find?

Seeds!

If you put the seed in the soil,
what will happen?

Reading Science

1 All the following are parts of a plant, **except–**

A roots.

B seed.

C stem.

D the Sun.

2 What part holds the plant before it grows?

A Leaves

B Stem

C Seed

D Roots

 **Reading Science**

3 What is the main function of the roots?

A To make food

B To bring water and food from the soil to the plant

C To carry water to the leaves

D To support the plant

4 What is the flower's job?

A To make seeds

B To water the plant

C To harvest the plant

D To weed the plant

# Reading Science

5 What happens when a student puts seeds in the soil?

A They are picked up and eaten.
B They hide from the Sun.
C They grow into new plants.
D Nothing happens.

Name: _____ Date: _____

Open-Ended-Response

1. Water pipes take water to different parts of your house.
   What parts of a plant are like water pipes?

   _____

   -

   _____

   Draw a picture of a plant.
   Label the plant parts that are like water pipes on the picture.

2. Leaves store food for plants. How do we store our food?
   _____

   We store our food in a -

   _____

Open-Ended-Response

3. A stem helps a plant to stand up.

   Draw and write about a time you made or used something that stands up.

Name: _____ Date: _____

Claim-Evidence-Reasoning

Scenario

Tara and Lauren are walking through a field of beautiful flowers. Tara pulls a flower from the soil and notices that the roots are long and moist. Lauren tells Tara that the roots are long because they hold the plant in the ground. Lauren also says the seeds in the flower will grow into a new plant if they are planted in the ground. Tara is excited to go home and tell her family about how interesting plants are. She hopes she can grow some plants in her backyard.

Prompt

Write a scientific explanation about which plant parts help a plant grow and survive.

Claim: _____

_____

_____

help plants grow and survive.

Evidence: Write how you know!

_____

_____

_____

_____

Draw how you know!

Parts of Animals

Name: _____

Date: _____

Graphic Organizer

Animal Parts

Directions

Record information on several different animals. Fill out the Graphic Organizer, using words and/or pictures describing how these body parts help an animal do different things. In addition, name one way humans copy the function of each part to do different things.

Ears

Fins

Tails

Legs

Eyes

Explore 1

Zoo Scavenger Hunt

Find an animal for each clue. Draw or write an explanation to support your answer.

Clue	Animal	I Know This Because...
Can climb to get food		
Eats meat		
Lives in a warm place		
Finds food in water		
Escapes danger quickly		

Explore 1

Draw an Animal

Write three body parts that your animal has and their functions.

1. _____

2. _____

3. _____

Name: _____ Date: _____

Explore 2

Animal Parts

Eyes

Eagles have very good eyesight. They have to be able to see well to help them catch their prey. Look at the picture of the rabbit that is posted in your classroom. Draw what the rabbit looks like in Box 1. Use your eagle's eyes (binoculars) to look at the picture of the rabbit again. Draw what the rabbit looks like in Box 2.

Box 1: Human Eyes	Box 2: Eagle Eyes

Ears

Connect the animal ear with the correct cup size. Circle which size of "ear" made it easiest to hear.

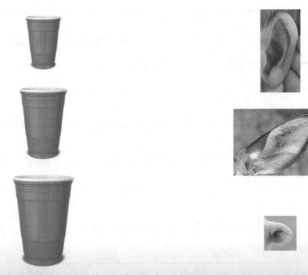

Explore 2

Feet

Draw your four animals in the boxes below. Discuss how each animal moves. Circle the body part each animal uses for movement.

Do all animals use feet to move? _____

Body Covering

Circle the type or types of body coverings that would keep animals warm and protect them from other animals.

Usefulness	Type of Body Covering			
Warmth	Fur	Feathers	Scales	Amphibian Skin
Protection	Fur	Feathers	Scales	Amphibian Skin

Which body covering provides an animal with both warmth and protection from things in their environment? _____

Explore 2

Teeth

Draw the best type of teeth for eating different foods. Put a check mark by the words that best describe each type of teeth.

Meat	
	☐ Sharp, pointy
	☐ Wide, round
	☐ Sharp, flat

Plants	
	☐ Sharp, pointy
	☐ Wide, round
	☐ Sharp, flat

Meat and Plants	
	☐ Sharp, pointy
	☐ Wide, round
	☐ Sharp, flat

Name: _____ Date: _____

 **Explore 2**

Animal Parts

Claim Evidence Reasoning

An animal's body parts help it survive.

What is one body part that helps animals survive?

Claim

An animal's _____help it survive, because...

_____

- -

_____
_____

- -

_____

Evidence

Draw a picture below that shows how your answer is true.

Name: _____ Date: _____

Explore 3

Animal Inventions

Record which animals you matched to each human invention.

Human Invention	Animal Part
Airplane	
Bike helmet	
Racing swimsuit	
Glow stick	
Bullet train	
Suction cups	

I know these human inventions copy animal parts because...

_____

_____

_____

_____

Name: _____ Date: _____

 **Explore 3**

Animal Inventions

Claim Evidence Reasoning

Prompt

How have animal structures helped humans?

Claim

Write a sentence that answers the question.

_____

_____

_____

_____

_____

Evidence

Draw a picture that shows your claim is true.

Name: _____ Date: _____

 **Explore 4**

Helpful Animal Parts

Draw how you think you will solve the problem.

[blank box]

What will you need to solve the problem? Draw or list the materials here.

[blank box]

Explore 4

Did your solution work? (yes or no)

Use the box below to draw how you could make your solution better.

```


```

If you have time, make changes to your solution to make it better.

Name: _____ Date: _____

 Linking Literacy

Three-Tab Notes

Cut along the dotted lines. Fold along the middle line. Record information from the text about each topic under the flap.

Protection

Food and Water

Movement

Name: _____ Date: _____

 **Linking Literacy**

Animal and Habitat Drawing

Draw a picture of one animal from the text in its habitat.

1. The animal protects itself by _____

_____

2. The animal gets food from _____

_____

3. The animal gets water from _____

_____

4. The animal moves by _____

_____

Name: _____ Date: _____

Reading Science

Bryce's Backyard Adventure

Reading Science
First Grade: Parts of Animals

Bryce is going on an animal adventure in his backyard. He grabs his binoculars, and out he goes!

He sees a lion. Bryce wonders why lions have such sharp teeth and claws.

Lions are meat eaters. They need sharp teeth and claws to help them hunt and tear the food they eat. What kind of things do you think the lion eats?

Reading Science

Bryce's guess is an antelope …

or a zebra.

Next, Bryce sees a giraffe. He wonders why it has such a long neck.

The giraffe's long neck helps him reach the leaves at the top of the trees. But it might make it hard to drink water!

Does the elephant have a long neck?

No, but he uses his trunk to get food.

Bryce has had an amazing adventure! Why can Bryce see so many animals in his backyard? Because he lives in Africa!

Reading Science

1 Where is Bryce going on his animal adventure?

    A   In his house

    B   In the patio

    C   In the front yard

    D   In the backyard

    E

2 Why do lions have sharp teeth and claws?

    A   To hunt and tear their food

    B   To run fast

    C   To open their mouths wide

    D   To smile

3 Meat eaters might eat–

A fruits.
B vegetables.
C zebras.
D plants.
E

4 Why does a giraffe have a long neck?

A To make him tall
B To reach the leaves at the top of the trees
C To look over all the other animals
D To breathe better

Reading Science

5 How does an elephant use its trunk?

A To get food
B As a back scratcher
C To move from place to place
D All of the above

Name: _____ Date: _____

 Open-Ended-Response

1. A pelican uses its pouch as a tool to scoop fish.

What tool do you use to scoop food?

_____

I use a ---

_____

2. A duck's feathers stay dry in the water.

What do you use to stay dry in the rain?

_____

I use a ---

_____

to stay dry in the rain.

Open-Ended-Response

3. You need to cross a river. Draw a picture and use words to show how you will do it.

_____

- -

_____

4. Now think of an animal who needs to cross a river. What will it use?

My animal is a(an) _____

The animal will use _____

Name: _____ Date: _____

Claim-Evidence-Reasoning

Scenario

A platypus has a flat tail like a beaver and webbed feet like a duck. These body parts help platypuses live in a water habitat.

Andrew has lots of gear in his pool bag for swimming. Andrew has goggles, flippers, and a snorkle!

Prompt

Which one of Andrew's toys is most like the platypus's feet?

Claim: _____

Andrew's- - - - - - - - - - - - - - - -
_____

are most like the platypus's feet.

Evidence: Write how you know!

_____
- - - - - - - - - - - - - - - - - - - -
_____
- - - - - - - - - - - - - - - - - - - -
_____
- - - - - - - - - - - - - - - - - - - -
_____
- - - - - - - - - - - - - - - - - - - -
_____

Draw how you know!

Plant Survival

Name: _____ Date: _____

Graphic Organizer

How Does a Plant Survive?

Plant Survival

Record different ways plants respond to the following changes in their environments in order to survive.

> Changes in Temperature

> Changes in Light

> Changes in Water
>
> Too much: Not enough:

> Other Organisms

Name: _____ Date: _____

 **Explore 1**

Data recording Table

Our Driving Question:
How do plants react to sunlight?

What We Need:
1 Small plant
Water

Procedure:
1. Get a plant from your teacher.
2. Go outside and find a safe, sunny place where the plant can be left for several days. A tabletop near a classroom window would work as well. Lay the plant on its side.
3. Record the date on the data table in the First Test section on page 2 and draw what your plant looks like while it is on its side.
4. Every 2 days, water your plant and observe how it has changed. Write the date in the next box in the First Test section on your data table on page 2 and draw what your plant looks like.
5. After you have made four observations, you are done with the first test.
6. For the second test, turn your plant over so that it is lying on its other side.
7. Continue to water, observe, and draw the plant every 2 days until you have made four more observations.

Explore 1

Growing Sideways

First Test	Date _____	Date _____
	Date _____	Date _____

Second Test	Date _____	Date _____
	Date _____	Date _____

Name: _____ Date: _____

 **Explore 1**

Growing Sideways

Claim Evidence Reasoning

Use what you have learned in the investigation to complete the sentence.

The plant turned and grew toward the _____

Write a sentence or draw a picture to show how you know the sentence is true.

_____

_____

_____

_____

 **Explore 2**

Growing Spuds

Part I

Draw what the potatoes look like BEFORE completing the experiment. Then make predictions. After 2 weeks, record what the potatoes look like AFTER.

Potatoes BEFORE	What I Think Will Happen	Potatoes AFTER
Potato in Refrigerator		
Potato Near Window		

Explore 2

Part II

Record what the potatoes look like each day for 2 weeks in the table below.

Week 1					
	Day 1	**Day 2**	**Day 3**	**Day 4**	**Day 5**
Potato in Refrigerator					
Potato near Window					

Week 2					
	Day 1	**Day 2**	**Day 3**	**Day 4**	**Day 5**
Potato in Refrigerator					
Potato near Window					

Name: _____ Date: _____

 **Explore 2**

Growing Spuds

Claim Evidence Reasoning

Use what you have learned in the investigation to complete the sentence.

_____ _____

Potatoes grow best in a -

_____ _____

environment.

Write a sentence or draw a picture to show how you know the sentence is true.

_____

- -

_____

- -

Name: _____ Date: _____

 # Linking Literacy

Plant Survival Notes

WHILE you read:

Listen to the STEMscopedia about how plants survive. Complete the sentences, using the information in the text.

1. In the winter, some plants stop _____ because they go **dormant.**

2. Winter is a difficult season for _____ as well as animals.

3. Many flowers bloom in _____ and some trees grow new leaves.

4. One new thing I learned about how plants survive is:

_____

_____

_____

_____

Name: _____   Date: _____

Linking Literacy
Post-Reading

Four-Corner Summary

Some plants survive cold temperatures by
_____
_____
_____

Other plants survive cold temperatures by
_____
_____
_____

Plant Survival

Another way plants survive cold temperatures is by
_____
_____
_____

Plants react to the Sun by
_____
_____
_____

Name: _____ Date: _____

Reading Science

What Plants Need

Reading Science
First Grade: Plant Survival

Jack and Max want to plant seeds. They have pots. They have seeds. They have sand. They have soil.

Jack plants his seed. He puts it in soil. Max plants his seed. He puts it in sand.

"Time to water," says Jack. "I will water it," says Max. Jack and Max water the seeds. Max puts his seed in his room. Jack puts his seed in a sunny window.

Jack waters his seed. Max forgets to water his seed. Jack checks his seed. His seed has sprouted. He sees a green stem. He sees a green leaf. It looks strong. Max's seed does not sprout.

"My seed is not growing," says Max.
"Did you water it?" asks Jack.
"I forgot," says Max.

"Your seed needs water. Your seed needs more sunlight," says Jack. "We will plant it in soil. The soil will help it grow healthy. We will put it in a sunny window."

Max and Jack plant a new seed.
They put it in soil. They put it in the sunny window. Max gives it water. He sees a plant.

He waters it. He keeps it in the window.
His plant is green and strong.
He keeps watering it. In a few weeks,
a bud grows, and a flower opens.

Reading Science

1 What does a plant need to survive?

  A A window
  B A pot
  C Sand
  D Water

2 Why didn't the seed grow in Max's room?

  A It was too bright in his room.
  B He forgot to water his plant.
  C His room needed more sunlight.
  D The seed did not grow.

 **Reading Science**

3 What is this story mostly about?

A Planting seeds in sand
B Why we plant seeds
C What is needed to plant a seed
D What plants need to live

4 Why did Jack's seed grow before Max's?

A He watered his plant every day.
B He put it in a sunny window.
C He planted his seed in soil.
D All of the above

Reading Science

5 What did Max learn about what plants need?

   A Plants need sand to grow.

   B Plants need sunlight and water to grow.

   C Plants do not need soil.

   D Plants do not need water.

   E

6 What is the author's purpose in writing this text?

   A To persuade the reader to plant seeds

   B To entertain the reader with a story about plants

   C To inform the reader about what plants need to grow.

   D To make the reader laugh

Reading Science

7 What could be another title for this selection?

   A "Max Learns a Lesson"
   B "The Seed That Didn't Grow"
   C "Seeds Need Water"
   D "Max and Jack Plant Seeds"

Reading Science

Name: _____ Date: _____

📖 Open-Ended-Response

1. Look at the picture.

   How do the spines (sharp points)on the cactus help it?

   _____

   The spines –

   _____

   –

   _____

   –

   _____

2. How do roots help a plant?

   _____

   The roots help the plant to – – – – – – – – – – – – – –

   _____

   –

   _____

   –

   _____

Open-Ended-Response

3. What are some things plants need to grow and survive?

Use words and pictures to show your answer.

_____

- -

_____

- -

_____

Claim-Evidence-Reasoning

Scenario

Mr. Davis bought a seed from the store. He brought it home and planted it in dry soil. The seed was not growing, so he decided to plant the seed in moist soil and place it near the window. Over time, the seed grew into a plant, which started leaning toward the window.

| Prompt | Thinking like a scientist, explain why the plant was able to grow in moist soil and why it leaned toward the window. |

Claim: The plant started growing and leaning because ...

_____

_____

_____

Evidence: Write how you know!   Draw how you know!

_____

_____

_____

_____

_____

Animal Survival

Name: _____ Date: _____

![Graphic Organizer logo] **Graphic Organizer**

Animal Survival Needs

Directions

Fill out the Graphic Organizer using words and/or pictures describing how animals survive using each of the five senses.

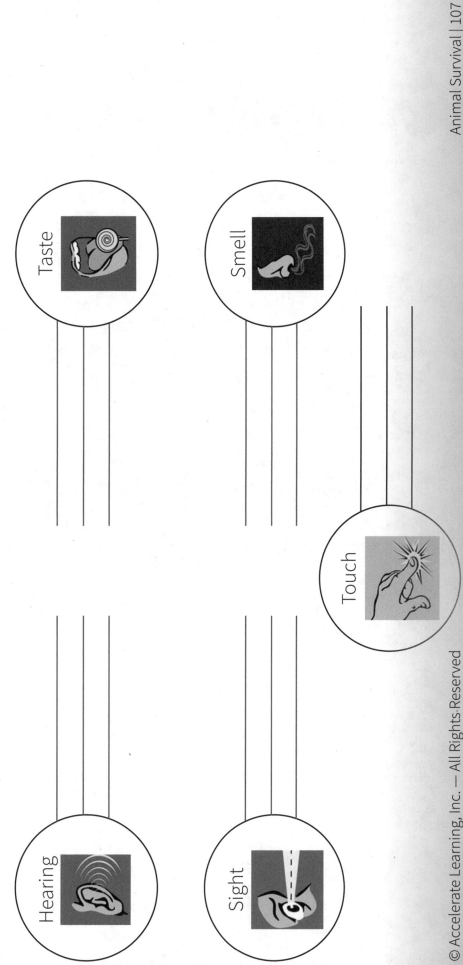

Name: _____ Date: _____

 **Explore 1**

Hmm...I'm hungry!

Directions:

Write the container number in the box and put a check mark in the correct column to show which scents smell like food and which ones do not. Record your observations.

Container Number	Smells Like Food	Does NOT Smell Like Food	Observations

Explore 1

Container Number	Smells Like Food	Does NOT Smell Like Food	Observations

Name: _____ Date: _____

 **Explore 1**

Hmm...I'm hungry!

Claim Evidence Reasoning

Thinking about today's activity, write or draw a scientific explanation about what sense you think people and animals can use to find food.

Claim

Animals and humans can use their sense of
to find food.

_____

- -

_____

Evidence

How do you know?

_____

- -

_____

- -

_____

Name: _____ Date: _____

 **Explore 2**

Survivor!

Glue your cards in the boxes below.

Draw a picture of how the animal uses its senses to survive.

Name: _____ Date: _____

Reading Science

Fur, Scales, and Teeth

Reading Science

First Grade: Animal Survival

Lily and Coral are sisters. They just finished looking at an animal book from their grandparents.

"Wow! There are animals of all different shapes and sizes," says Lily.
"I know," says Coral. "They all look so different."

"Did you see all the different kinds of fur?" asks Coral.
"Yes," says Lily. "The tiger's fur has stripes. It blends in and hides in the forest."

Reading Science

"Zebras have stripes, too," says Coral, "but their stripes help them hide in the herd.

"The arctic hare has fur that changes color. It is brown in the summer to match the ground. It turns white in the winter to hide on the snow," says Coral."

Lily points at a parrot. "The parrot has brightly colored feathers. This makes it easy for other parrots in the jungle to see it."

"What about the animals that have scales?" asks Coral. "They live in places without a lot of water. Their scales protect them from the heat and the cold."

Reading Science

Lily holds up a picture of a lion roaring. "Look at the sharp teeth in the lion's mouth. He needs them to hunt and eat."

Coral turns the page to a horse. "Horses have flat teeth, because they eat grass."

"I like giraffes," says Lily. "They have long necks to reach up into trees for leaves."

"And they have long tongues. They use them to pull the leaves off the branches," giggles Coral.

"Elephants can also reach up into the trees to get their food, using their trunks," says Lily.

"Did you know that an elephant's trunk is his nose?" asks Coral.
"They also use their noses to drink water and give themselves a shower."

"I wish I had feet like a duck when we go to the swimming pool," says Lily.
"I could swim faster than you.

Coral laughs. "And I wish I had claws like a cat when we climb trees. I could get to the top faster than you."

"Okay, my two silly girls. I wish you would be quick like rabbits and go get ready for bed," says Mom.

Lily and Coral hop out of the room like two little bunnies. faster than you."

Reading Science

1 What is the theme of this text?

A Lily and Coral are very lucky to have a new book from their grandparents.

B Lily and Coral have the same bedtime.

C Animals' bodies have many different ways to help them survive.

D Lily and Coral like to swim and climb trees.

Reading Science

2 Why do some animals have scales?

   A The scales protect them from the environment.

   B The scales are brightly colored to warn other animals that they are poisonous.

   C The scales can be used as weapons.

   D Scales are fun to touch.

3 Giraffes use their long necks and elephants use their trunks to–

   A reach their food in trees.

   B drink water.

   C wave to their friends.

   D give themselves a shower

4 Both tigers and zebras have stripes to–

   A look different from other animals.
   B hide from other animals.
   C look alike.
   D look pretty.

5 How might the reader think Lily and Coral feel about their new book?

   A They feel bored with the book.
   B They wish it were a different book.
   C They don't like the book.
   D They like their new book.

Name: _____ Date: _____

 # Open-Ended-Response

1. A wolf lives in a very cold place. What helps the wolf stay warm?

_____

- -

_____

helps the wolf stay warm.

2. Look at the pictures.

How are fingers and bird beaks the same?
They are both used to _____

_____

- -

_____

_____

- -

_____

Open-Ended-Response

3. Imagine you can be an animal for a day! What animal would you be?

_____

I would be a(n) -

_____

Draw and write how you would protect yourself from enemies.

_____

- -

_____

- -

Name: _____ Date: _____

Claim-Evidence-Reasoning

Animal Survival

Scenario

An owl is sitting on a branch. Nearby, a rabbit makes a rustling noise as it moves through the brush. The owl turns its head toward the rabbit. Once the owl detects the rabbit's motion, it swoops in to claim its prey.

Prompt

Thinking like a scientist, what body parts provide information to the owl to help it catch its prey?

Claim:

The owl uses its _____ and _____ to catch its prey.

Evidence: Write how you know!

_____

_____

_____

_____

_____

_____

Draw how you know!

Animal Survival | 127

Plant Trait Inheritance and Variation

Name: _____ Date: _____

 Graphic Organizer

Plant Offspring

Using the chart below, list some characteristics a plant offspring might inherit and those it might not.

Traits an Offspring Might Inherit	Draw and Label These Traits
	Where do these traits come from?

Name: _____ Date: _____

 **Explore 1**

Plant Babies

Directions

1. With your partner, go to each bag and randomly select which characteristics your plant will inherit from its parents.
2. Choose only one item from each bag, without looking, so that you have one flower, one center, one stem, and one leaf set.
3. Assemble and glue your plant's parts to the white paper to create the offspring.
4. Post your offspring in the location chosen by your teacher.
5. As a class, record how many offspring showed each trait in the table below, using tally marks.

Long Stem	**Short Stem**	**Red Petals**	**Pink Petals**	**Orange Center**	**Yellow Center**	**Dark-Green Leaves**	**Light-Green Leaves**

Are all the offspring exactly the same?

_____

Why do you think they all look a little different? _____

_____

_____

_____

Name: _____ Date: _____

 **Explore 1**

Plant Babies

Claim Evidence Reasoning

Write or **draw** a scientific explanation to show if you think the offspring of two plants will always look exactly like its parents.

Claim: Check all that are true.

The plants' offspring —
- ☐ will always look exactly like one parent.
- ☐ can sometimes look exactly like one parent.
- ☐ can look a little different from one parent.

Evidence: Write a sentence and draw a picture to prove the statements you choose above are true.

_____

- -

_____

- -

_____

Name: _____ Date: _____

Explore 2

Who Are My Parents?

Observe the characteristics of the offspring cards, and discuss them with your group. Decide which two parents each offspring came from, and record your information below.

	Parent 1	**Parent 2**
Plant 1		
Plant 2		
Plant 3		
Plant 4		
Plant 5		
Plant 6		

How did you know which flowers were from the parents of Plant 1?

_____

_____

_____

How did you decide which plants were the parents of each offspring?

_____

_____

_____

Name: _____ Date: _____

 **Explore 2**

Plant Babies

Claim Evidence Reasoning

Write or **draw** a scientific explanation to tell which two plants are the parents of Plant 5.

Claim: Finish the sentence below.

The parents of Plant 5 are ...

_____

_ _

_____

Evidence: Write how you know!

_____

_ _

_____

_ _

_____

Draw how you know!

Name: _____ Date: _____

 # Linking Literacy

Trait or Variation Sort

Directions: Cut out the boxes at the bottom of the page. Sort them on the chart to show if the trait comes from a parent plant or if it is a variation that may be seen in offspring.

Inherited Traits: Characteristics of Plants and Animals Passed Down from Parent to Offspring	Variation: Offspring Can Be Different from a Parent; Difference Can Be in Stripe, Pattern, Color, Size, or Shape

Leaf size and shape	Size of a tomato	Color of a daffodil	Has a stem
Ivy climbs a wall	Number of branches	Number of flowers	Size of a plant

Name: _____ Date: _____

Linking Literacy

Draw and Explain

Directions: Look at the parent plant card. Glue it in the box below. Think about traits and how offspring and parents can be similar. Draw and label a picture of a plant that could be the offspring of the plant on your card. Then, explain how they are alike and different.

> **Glue the parent plant card here.**

My offspring plant is like the parent plant because _ _ _ _ _ _ _ _ _ _ _ _ _ _ _ _ _

_ _

and different because _

Name: _____ Date: _____

Reading Science

Plant Traits

Reading Science

First Grade: Plant Trait Inheritance and Variation

You see a bunch of roses. You wonder why they all look the same. You notice they are all the same color. They are all the same shape and have thorns. Plants look the same because of inherited traits.

Inherited traits are passed down from the parent plant to the young plant. A parent cannot choose which traits it wants to pass down. It just happens!

Reading Science

All plants have seeds. If you plant these seeds, a new plant will grow. Some plants make fruit. Some plants make flowers. Some plants have both fruit and flowers. The new plant that grows will have the same fruit or flower as the parent plant. The young fruit or flower will be the same color and shape.

The young plant will also have the same shape and the same-size leaves as the parent plant. If a parent plant has small leaves, its young will also have small leaves.

A parent plant also passes on its root system to its young. The young plant will have the same-size root system as its parent. If the parent has a short and wide root system, so will the young.

Reading Science

Even though young plants are very much like their parent, they may also differ in many ways. Compared to their parent, young plants may have slight color differences in their flower.

The size of a young plant's leaves may be the same, but the number of leaves could vary. So could the number of flower petals. Some plants may have more or fewer leaves or petals.

Young plants' roots can also be different from their parents. Not every young plant has the same number of roots as its parent. Some have more, and some have less. The root system is about the same size in parents and young plants. Not all roots will be the exact same length.

Young plants can also vary in height. Plants will be similar to their parents' height. They will not be the exact same height.

Young plants are very much like their parents, but they are also different in many ways!

1 What is slide 6 mostly about?

A Plants have the exact same length of roots.

B Young plants' roots differ from their parents'.

C Young plants are different in height.

D Parent plant roots are exactly the same.

 **Reading Science**

2 What is the most important information about plants from this selection that the reader could tell someone?

   A Plants have seeds.
   B Plants cannot choose the traits they pass on to their young.
   C Parent plants and their young are alike and different in many ways.
   D Plants are important to nature.

3 All the following are examples of inherited traits, except–

   A the size of the root system.
   B the color of the flower.
   C the size of the leaf.
   D the number of leaves or thorns.

4 The reader can conclude that a young plant–

A looks very different from its parent.

B looks exactly like its parent.

C looks similar to its parent, with some differences.

D has a different root system than its parent.

Name: _____ Date: _____

 Open-Ended-Response

1. What is the same and different about these corn plants?.

They both have
_____

- -

_____

They have different
_____

- -

_____

2. What is the same and different about these cactus plants?

They both have
_____

- -

_____

They have different
_____

- -

_____

Open-Ended-Response

3. The picture shows a leaf from an oak tree.

What will the leaves of the baby oak tree look like?

Use words and a picture to show your answer.

Name: _____ Date: _____

Claim-Evidence-Reasoning

Scenario

At the beginning of spring, Laura and her family planted a rose garden in their backyard. The roses grew and produced beautiful yellow and pink rosebuds. The next spring, the family noticed new rosebushes that the family did not plant. They realized that the roses they planted last year had produced offspring.

Parent 1   Parent 2

Offspring 1   Offspring 2   Offspring 3

Prompt   Which flowers could be the offspring of the yellow and pink parent roses? You can list more than one.

Claim: Offspring _ _ _ _ _ _ _ _ _ _ _ _ _ _ _ could be the offspring of the yellow

and pink parent roses.

Evidence: Write how you know!

_____

_____

_____

_____

_____

California Instructional Segment

Take Action!

Design a rattle that can be attached to Sammy.

• Rattlesnakes use their rattles to warn people and animals to stay away.

    • Many things make sounds.

Draw Sammy's new rattle to attach to his tail!

Build Sammy's new rattle to attach to his tail!

Name: _____

Date: _____

California Instructional Segment

Our Mission:

A Rattle for Sammy

California Instructional Segment

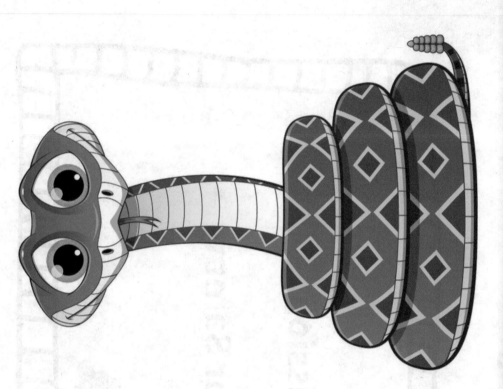

Sammy is a rattlesnake.

He rattles his tail to let others know he's there.

California Instructional Segment

One day, Sammy tried to warn people that they were getting too close.

The people didn't hear him, so Sammy crawled into a bush.

The bush had thorns!

Sammy got a thorn stuck in his rattle. Ouch!

Now his rattle isn't working.

California Instructional Segment

Sammy needs a new rattle so he can let others know where he is.

Can you help make a new rattle for Sammy?

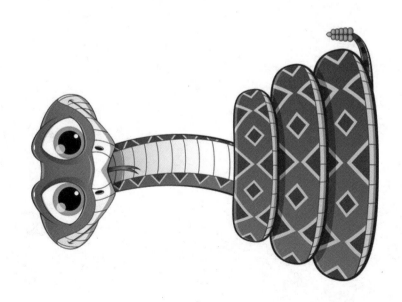

Sound

Name: _____ Date: _____

Graphic Organizer

Good Vibrations

Directions

Draw examples of how sound can make matter vibrate and how vibrating matter can make sound.

| Sounds Make Matter Vibrate | Vibrating Matter Makes Sound |

Name: _____ Date: _____

 # Hook

Laser Show
Class Anchor Chart

What I Noticed

Laser on the Ceiling	Tuning Fork When Tapped
Laser Light with Light Tap	Laser Light with Hard Tap

Name: _____ Date: _____

Explore 1

Sound Stations

Observations	Station 1	Station 2	Station 3	Station 4
What did I see before the sound?				
What did I hear?				
Did anything move?				

How is sound made?

_____

What body part vibrates when we talk?

_____

Name: _____ Date: _____

Claim-Evidence-Reasoning

Scenario

There are many different types of sounds. There are loud and quiet sounds. There are high- and low-pitched sounds. When you hit a drum, it makes a sound. If the drum is close to a cymbal, the cymbal will also make a sound without anything even hitting it.

Prompt Thinking like a scientist, how do the drum and the cymbal make sound?

Claim: The reason the drum and cymbal make sound is because of:

_____

_ .

_____

Evidence: Write how you know!

_____

_ _

_____

_ _

_____

_ _

_____

Draw how you know!

Name: _____ Date: _____

Explore 2

Sound System

What happens when different objects are used to create sound?

Plan it!
Circle one object that will be different from the example basic sound system.

Cup	Spoon	String

- -

Test it!
Construct your system with the new object.
The new system made a —

☐ **louder sound.**　　　　☐ **lower sound.**

☐ **softer sound.**　　　　☐ **higher sound.**

- -

Watch what happens!

Explore 2

Wrap It Up!
Draw what you see and hear!

Name: _____ Date: _____

Linking Literacy

Which Will Make a Sound?

BEFORE you read:

Circle the objects that would make a sound.

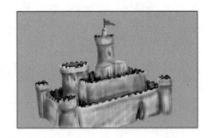

Name: _____ Date: _____

 Linking Literacy

3-2-1 Sound

After reading the text silently, complete the 3-2-1 chart, using information that you learned. Be prepared to share your findings with the class.

3	**Three facts you know about sound from the reading.**
2	**Two examples of sounds that were not in the reading.**
1	**One question you still have about sound.**

Name: _____ Date: _____

Reading Science

Sound

Reading Science
First Grade: Sound

How are sounds made? When an object is hit or dropped, it moves back and forth quickly. This is known as *vibration*.

If you hit a drum with a stick, the drum will **vibrate** and cause the sound that your ears hear.

Reading Science

Place some rice on the drum, and hit it with a stick. The rice will bounce on the drum, causing a sound.

Your mouth also makes sound. When you play a kazoo, you feel your lips vibrate. It makes them feel funny. They move back and forth rapidly.

When you speak, you can feel your voice box vibrate. The vibrations allow you to speak.

We hear sound through speakers when we watch a movie. Place your hand on a speaker, and you will feel it move.

Reading Science

When you turn the sound up, the speakers bounce more. The bigger vibrations cause the sound to be louder.

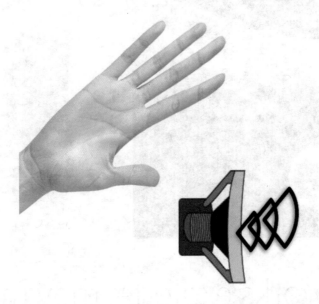

You can even hear sound below water in the swimming pool. That's because sound is able to pass through liquid.

Sound also passes through solids and gases. Many objects have the ability to carry sound.

When fireworks explode, they make a loud noise in the sky. You can feel it in your chest.

Sometimes sounds make objects move.
When the firework explodes, it causes
you to move. That's why you can feel
them when they are loud.

Sound makes objects move.
We need vibrations to hear sounds.
Without vibrations, we would hear nothing!

Reading Science

1 What does it mean to vibrate?

A Sound
B Move quickly back and forth
C Hear
D Run very fast

2 The passage explains that sound can pass through all the following, except–

A solids.
B gases.
C outer space.
D liquids.

Reading Science

3 This passage is mostly about–

 A how a kazoo makes your mouth vibrate.
 B how to use a ruler to make sound.
 C how to make objects move.
 D how sound is made through vibrations.

4 If a student's mom tells them to turn the TV down a little, the speakers will make–

 A the same size vibration.
 B smaller vibrations.
 C bigger vibrations.
 D no vibration.

5 A student's brother is playing loud music in his room. The student sees a picture on the wall start to move. What makes the picture move?

A The student's brother
B Running in the house
C The student's mom's voice
D The loud music

Name: _____ Date: _____

Open-Ended-Response

1. If you hold your hand on your throat while you hum, what do you feel?

    _____

    I feel -

    _____

2. What causes sound?

    _____

    -

    _____

    cause sound.

3. Draw what you can do to make sound.

Name: _____ Date: _____

Claim-Evidence-Reasoning

Scenario

There are many different types of sounds. There are loud and quiet sounds. There are high- and low-pitched sounds. When you hit a drum, it makes a sound. If the drum is close to a cymbal, the cymbal will also make a sound without anything even hitting it.

Prompt Thinking like a scientist, how do the drum and the cymbal make sound?

Claim: The reason the drum and cymbal make sound is because of:

_____

_____ .

_____

Evidence: Write how you know!

Draw how you know!

_____

_____

_____

_____

_____

_____

_____

Communication

Name: _____

Date: _____

Graphic Organizer

Sending Messages

Directions

Draw or write ways to communicate using light and sound.

Name: _____ Date: _____

 **Explore 1**

Talking with Lights

My Morse Code Message
(it can be no longer than five letters.)

My Partner's Code Message

Name: _____ Date: _____

 **Explore 1**

Talking with Lights

Claim Evidence Reasoning

Think about today's activity. Now, write and draw a scientific explanation about how Morse code can be used to communicate.

Claim

Morse code can send a message by using...

_____

- -

_____

Evidence

Draw and label a picture that shows how you know the sentence above is true.

Name: _____ Date: _____

 **Explore 2**

What Did We Hear?

Plan it! — Pick three objects.

3 x 5 note card	9 x 12 card stock	18 x 24 bendable poster board
paper towel roll	straw	plastic cup with the bottom cut out

Sound Amplifier 1: _____

Sound Amplifier 2: _____

Sound Amplifier 3: _____

Write three words or phrases.

Word or phrase 1: _____

Word or phrase 2: _____

Word or phrase 3: _____

Test it!

10 feet away   20 feet away

- -

Hear what happens!

Explore 2

Wrap It Up! — Write what you heard!

10 Feet
Sound Amplifier 1
Sound Amplifier 2
Sound Amplifier 3

20 Feet
Sound Amplifier 1
Sound Amplifier 2
Sound Amplifier 3

Name: _____ Date: _____

Explore 2

What Did We Hear?

Claim Evidence Reasoning

Think about the materials you used to try to make the sound louder. Using simple materials, what communication device could people use to be able to make their voices heard far away? Answer below and make sure you can support your claim with evidence.

_____

_____

_____

_____

_____

_____

_____

Draw how you know!

Name: _____ Date: _____

 **Explore 3**

Let's Talk!

Draw how you think you will solve the problem.

What will you need to solve the problem? Draw or list the materials here.

Explore 3

Did your solution work?   (yes or no)

Use the box below to draw how you could make your solution better.

If you have time, make changes to your solution to make it better.

Name: _____ Date: _____

Linking Literacy

Senses and Communication

As your teacher reads from the STEMscopedia, think about which senses are used in each method of communication. Draw a line to connect each method of communication with the sense or senses it uses.

Telephone

Television

Computer

Sight

Smell

Taste

Hearing

Touch

Name: _____ Date: _____

 **Linking Literacy**

Write a Letter

AFTER you read:

Use the postcard below to write a letter to a friend in another class at your school. Use the postcard to communicate with your friend about your favorite food.

Dear _____,

_____

- -

_____

_____

- -

_____

_____

- -

_____

From, _____

To: _____

Teacher:_____

Grade:_____

Name: _____ Date: _____

Reading Science

The Cell Phone

Reading Science
First Grade: Communication

Jake was sad. He missed his grandparents. It had been a long time since he had seen them. He lived in Texas. His grandma and grandpa lived in Florida. Jake got an award at school. He wanted to tell his grandparents.

Jake asked his mom if he could call his grandma and grandpa. Jake's mom let him use her cell phone. Jake called the number. There was no answer.

Reading Science

Jake asked his mom if there was another way. She told Jake about text messages. She let Jake send a text message. Jake sent a text to his grandma's phone. His eyes got brighter. This was the first text message he had sent. Jake waited.

The phone beeped. There was a text from Jake's grandma. She could not wait to hear about his award.

Jake wanted to show them his award. His mom said they could take a video. Jake could hold his award. He could also speak to his grandparents. Jake's mom used her cell phone. She took the video.

Jake and his mom sent the video to his grandparents. They used her cell phone. They sent it by email from her phone. Her phone could do a lot!

Reading Science

Jake couldn't wait for his grandparents to see his video. He was so excited to hear from them. Soon, his mom's phone beeped. Thanks to cell phones, he did not have to wait too long.

1 The author wrote this passage mainly to–

A give information about

B communication.

C tell an entertaining story about

D a kid who communicated with his grandparents.

2 The reader can tell that Jake–

A didn't know how to take a video.

B was shy to speak to his grandparents.

C was excited to share his news with his grandparents.

D had sent a text message before.

3 The phrase, *his eyes got brighter*, tells the reader that Jake felt–

    A confused.
    B excited.
    C upset.
    D bored.

4 Why did Jake want to call his grandparents?

    A He wanted to try to send a text message.
    B He wanted to show off his award.
    C He wanted to show them his video.
    D He wanted to use his mom's phone.

Reading Science

5 What way was Jake **not** able to reach his grandparents?

A Video

B Email

C Text message

D Letter

Name: _____ Date: _____

Open-Ended-Response

1. Sirens warn people of danger.

    Draw a picture to show other ways we use sound.

```



```

2. What do you have that uses light and sound to communicate?

    I have a _

 **Open-Ended-Response**

3. How are light and sound used in your favorite video game or TV program?

Use words and a picture.

Name: _____ Date: _____

Claim-Evidence-Reasoning

Scenario

TJ and his dad were walking along the shore. TJ saw a ship on the ocean. He also heard a loud horn and saw flashing lights. They were not near a road, so he wondered what it could be. His dad told him it was a lighthouse warning a ship that it was close to land.

Prompt Using scientific reasoning, explain how lighthouses communicate with ships and boats.

Claim: Lighthouses use _ _ _ _ _ _ _ _ _ _ and _ _ _ _ _ _ _ _ _ _ to communicate

with ships and boats.

Evidence: Write how you know!

_____
_ _ _ _ _ _ _ _ _ _ _ _ _ _ _ _ _ _
_____
_ _ _ _ _ _ _ _ _ _ _ _ _ _ _ _ _ _
_____
_ _ _ _ _ _ _ _ _ _ _ _ _ _ _ _ _ _
_____
_ _ _ _ _ _ _ _ _ _ _ _ _ _ _ _ _ _

Draw how you know!

Protecting the Young

Graphic Organizer

How Animals Protect Their Young

Write the name of an animal in the first rectangle. List three ways this animal protects its young.

Animal

Animal

Animal

Name: _____ Date: _____

 **Explore 1**

My Needs Charades

Draw one matching pair.

How did you know it was a match?

_____

- -

_____

- -

_____

How were you able to communicate your need without making a sound?

_____

- -

_____

- -

_____

 **Explore 1**

My Needs Charades

Claim Evidence Reasoning

Write and **draw** a scientific explanation about how parents meet the needs of their offspring.

Claim: Complete the following sentence.

Parents help meet their offspring's needs by ...

_____

_____

_____

Evidence: Describe an example of your claim and draw a picture of it.

_____

_____

_____

Name: _____ Date: _____

 **Explore 2**

Protecting Your Young

Animal: _____

Draw a picture of the animal and its young that you researched.

Write three ways your animal protects its young. Be ready to share these with the class.

Name: _____ Date: _____

 **Linking Literacy**

Who Makes the Rules?

Who makes the rules at school and at home?	How do rules help us at school? At home? On the playground?
Why do we have rules?	What would happen if we didn't have rules or if people didn't follow the rules?

Name: _____ Date: _____

Linking Literacy

Protecting Their Young

WHILE you read:

Pick one animal from the STEMscopedia and illustrate how the parent protects their young.

[drawing box]

Write what is happening in the picture in the space below.

_____

The -- protects its young by

_____

_____

Linking Literacy

Exit Ticket

Exit Ticket	Why would opossum and scorpion mothers let their babies ride on their backs?
	How does seaweed help sea otters?
	What might happen if a person or animal were to get too close to a bird's nest with eggs inside?

Exit Ticket	Why would opossum and scorpion mothers let their babies ride on their backs?
	How does seaweed help sea otters?
	What might happen if a person or animal were to get too close to a bird's nest with eggs inside?

Name: _____ Date: _____

Reading Science

Mom to the Rescue

Reading Science
First Grade: Protecting the Young

A baby elephant is born. Its mother feeds the baby milk. She makes sure the baby has food.

Elephants are born into a herd. A herd is a family. The baby elephant has aunts and grandmas that also act like mothers to the baby.

The mother teaches the baby elephant. She and the herd train the baby with their trunks.

It helps them learn what is right and what is wrong.

Mother elephants show love to their babies. They gently touch their babies with their tusks.

Mothers stay by their babies for years. They protect them.
The young elephant needs its mother's love.

Mother elephants also teach their young to find food

The young elephant watches the other elephants. It **mimics** their actions.

A young elephant sees another elephant playing with water.

The elephant is sucking up water in its trunk and spraying it on others. The young elephant does the same. Herds of elephants protect their young.

The herd circles around any young elephants. This is to guard them.

The herd stands close together. If they face any hunters, the young elephants hide in the middle.

The elephants are a strong group. A lion tries to get to the young elephants, but it can't. The elephants block the lion.

Mother elephants are great protectors.

They make sure their babies have food and love. They teach their young. They fight off hunters to protect their young. Baby elephants need their mothers to survive.

1 What words help the reader know what **mimic** means?

   A *Spraying it on others*
   B *Sucking up water in its trunk*
   C *Does the same*
   D *Find food*

2 What could be another title for this passage?

   A "Baby Elephants"
   B "Mother Elephants"
   C "Moms Protect Young"
   D "Elephant Herds"

Reading Science

3 The reader can infer that baby elephants–

   A protect themselves.
   B like to play.
   C help their mom.
   D eat plants.

4 The author wrote this to–

   A tell the reader how baby
   B elephants eat.
   C persuade the reader to save elephants.
   D inform the reader about moms protecting
       their young.
   E tell a story about elephants.

5 Elephants protect their young in all these ways, **except–**

A feeding them.

B playing with them.

C saving them from lions.

D training.

6 The elephant **herd** is–

A a party.

B a family.

C a team.

D a rock group.

Name: _____ Date: _____

 Open-Ended-Response

1. A baby kangaroo stays in its mother's pouch.

   How does this help the baby?

   The pouch helps to

   _____

   _ _ _ _ _ _ _ _ _ _ _ _ _ _ _ _ _ _

   _____

   _

   _____

2. A mother opossum carries her babies on her back. Why?

   The mother wants to

   _____

   _ _ _ _ _ _ _ _ _ _ _ _ _ _ _ _ _ _

   _____

   _

   _____

Open-Ended-Response

3. Parents protect their young. How were you protected when you were a baby?

Show your answer with words and a picture.

Claim-Evidence-Reasoning

Scenario

Kelly has been watching a family of birds in a nest in her backyard. She sees the adult bird fly away and come back a few times each day. She hears the baby birds chirping and sees them open their mouths wide when the adult bird comes back. She wonders how the bird knows when to come back.

Prompt   How does a baby bird let its parent know it needs something?

Claim: A baby bird _ _ _ _ _ _ _ _ _ _ _ _ _ to let its parent know it needs something.
             _____

Evidence: Write how you know!

_____

_____

_____

_____

Animal Trait inheritance and Variation

257

Name: _____ Date: _____

 Graphic Organizer

Why Do I Look like My Parents?

Animal Inheritance

Draw or find pictures of an adult animal. List the traits the animal's offspring might inherit from the adult animal. Then list some traits that the animal's offspring might not inherit.

Adult Animal	Traits an Offspring Might Inherit	Traits an Offspring Might NOT Inherit

Adult Animal	Traits an Offspring Might Inherit	Traits an Offspring Might NOT Inherit

Adult Animal	Traits an Offspring Might Inherit	Traits an Offspring Might NOT Inherit

Name: _____ Date: _____

 **Explore 1**

Bugs!

The **body size** will be _____, just like the _____ bug.

The **body shape** will be a _____, just like the _____ bug.

The **body color** will be _____, just like the _____ bug.

The **eye shape** will be _____, just like the _____ bug.

The **eye color** will be _____, just like the _____ bug.

The **antennae** will be _____, just like the _____ bug.

The **tail** will be _____, just like the _____ bug.

The **wings** will be _____, just like the _____ bug.

The **legs** will be _____, just like the _____ bug.

Bug Drawing

Draw a sibling bug from another group.

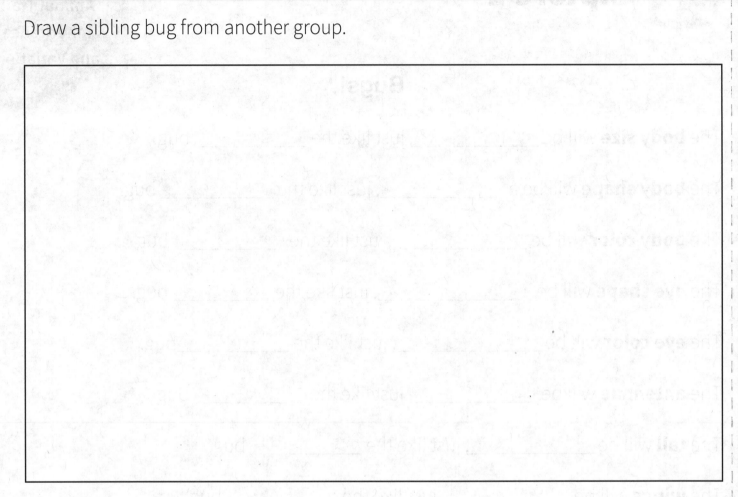

Name: _____ Date: _____

Explore 1

Bugs!

Claim Evidence Reasoning

Claim

Young animals look like their _____ - - - - - - - - - - - - - - but none of _____

them look exactly the _____ - - - - - - - - - - - - - . _____

Evidence

List two pieces of evidence from the activity that show you know the sentence above is true.

1. _____
   _____
   _____

2. _____
   _____
   _____

Explore 1

Are You My Parents?

Glue the picture of the parent animals here.	**Glue the picture of the baby here.**
Traits from Mom Dog	**Traits from Dad Dog**
_____	_____
_____	_____
_____	_____
_____	_____

Glue the picture of the parent animals here.	Glue the picture of the baby here.
Traits from Mom Dog	**Traits from Dad Dog**
_____	_____
_____	_____
_____	_____
_____	_____
_____	_____

Explore 1

Glue the picture of the parent animals here.	**Glue the picture of the baby here.**
Traits from Mom Dog	**Traits from Dad Dog**
_____ _____ _____ _____ _____	_____ _____ _____ _____ _____

Name: _____ Date: _____

Linking Literacy

Think about the story "The Ugly Duckling."

How could the mother duck tell which ones were her babies and which one hatched from an egg that accidentally rolled into her nest?

What about geese and ducks is similar? What is different?

Name: _____ Date: _____

Linking Literacy

3-2-1 Notes

WHILE you read:

Complete the table below:

3 Facts about Animal Traits and Variations	
2 Examples of Animal Traits or Variations	
1 Question You Still Have about Animal Traits and Variations	

Name: _____ Date: _____

Linking Literacy

Answer Those Questions!

AFTER you read: Copy your question from the during-reading activity in one of the boxes on the left. Ask two classmates what questions they still have, and record them in the other two boxes on the left. Work together to write in the boxes on the right reasonable answers based on the information from the text and additional classroom resources.

Questions	Answers
1	
2	
3	

Name: _____ Date: _____

Reading Science

From Pup to Dog

Reading Science

First Grade: Animal Trait Inheritance and Variation

Reading Science

Biscuit was Sally's dog. Biscuit just had five puppies. Sally was so excited to see the new pups! Sally saw that all the pups had fur. Biscuit had yellow fur.

Some of the pups had yellow fur. Some of the pups had spots around their eyes. Not all of the pups looked the same. "Why are they all different?" Sally asked her mom.

Sally's mom told her that young animals get traits from their parents. **Traits** are things that are the same among the same kind of animal. Traits that are passed from parents to their young are called *inherited traits*.

"Puppies have fur because their parents have fur," said Sally's mom. "They also have four legs, two ears, two eyes, and a nose. These traits were passed down from their parents. Young animals inherit some traits from their parents."

"What else do they get from their parents?" Sally wanted to know. "Puppies also get the way their body is built from their parents. If parents have a long tail, then the puppies may also have a long tail.

"If a parent is a kind dog, it may also pass that trait on to its young. Sometimes, the way an animal behaves can also be passed down from parent to child."

Reading Science

"Wow," said Sally. "I didn't know all these traits came from the parents. What can be different?"

"Their eye and hair color can **vary** a little," replied her mom. "Biscuit has yellow fur because her parents had yellow fur. Biscuit is passing that trait to her young."

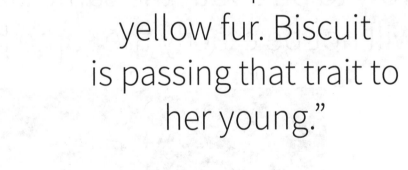

"Some are different. Look at the spots. Young animals are very much like their parents. They are not exactly the same.

"Some of Biscuit's pups have spots, and their fur is not all the exact same color. The pups will grow to be about the same size as Biscuit. They will not be exactly the same height or weight."

 **Reading Science**

"Wow! These puppies are alike but different! They are so cute!" exclaimed Sally as she watched Biscuit and her new pups.

1 Which sentence tells the reader that Sally was curious?

A "Wow," said Sally.

B "What else do they get from their parents?" Sally wanted to know.

C "They are so cute!"

D "These puppies are alike but different!"

2 What would be another good title for this selection?

A "Sally's Day"

B "Biscuit's Puppies"

C "Puppies Are Born"

D "Sally's Exciting Day"

3 What would mean the same as trait in this selection?

A Similar among a group

B Different among a group

C A touch

D A dog

4 What would be a trait that a human would get from their parents?

A A chipped or broken tooth

B How tall they are

C What they like to eat

D The clothes they wear

5 What would be a trait that an animal may have that varies from its parent?

A Its number of legs
B Its number of eyes
C Its eye color
D Its number of ears

6 What word(s) helps the reader know what the word vary means?

A Hair color
B Different
C Yellow fur
D Spots

Name: _____ Date: _____

📖 Open-Ended-Response

1. Observe the animals in the picture. How are they alike and different?

One way they are alike is

_____

- -

_____

One way they are different is

_____

- -

_____

2. Looking at this puppy, describe what you think the mother's ears and legs might look like.

The mother's ears might look

_____

- -

_____

The mother's legs might look

_____

- -

_____

Open-Ended-Response

3. Most baby animals look like their parents. Draw a picture of a baby animal and its parents to show how they look alike. Use pictures and words in your answer.

Name: _____ Date: _____

Claim-Evidence-Reasoning

Scenario

Timmy saw some kittens with their mother in the park. He noticed the kittens were mostly the same color as her, but one was not. He wondered where the other color came from.

Prompt   Thinking like a scientist, where do you think the other color of fur came from?

Claim: The other color of fur came from _____ .
_____

Evidence: Write how you know!

_____
_____
_____
_____
_____
_____
_____

Draw how you know!

Name: _____ Date: _____

 California Instructional Segment

Take Action!

Design a night-light that will project shadows and images on the wall in different colors.

- Light travels in straight lines.
- If all the light is blocked, the shadow is black.
- If no light is blocked, the light is white.
- If some of the light is blocked by something that is colored, the image will be in that color.

Design your new night-light cover.

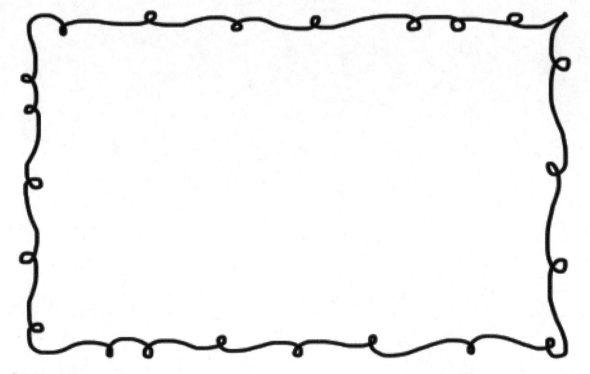

 Build your new night-light cover!

Name: _____

Date: _____

California Instructional Segment

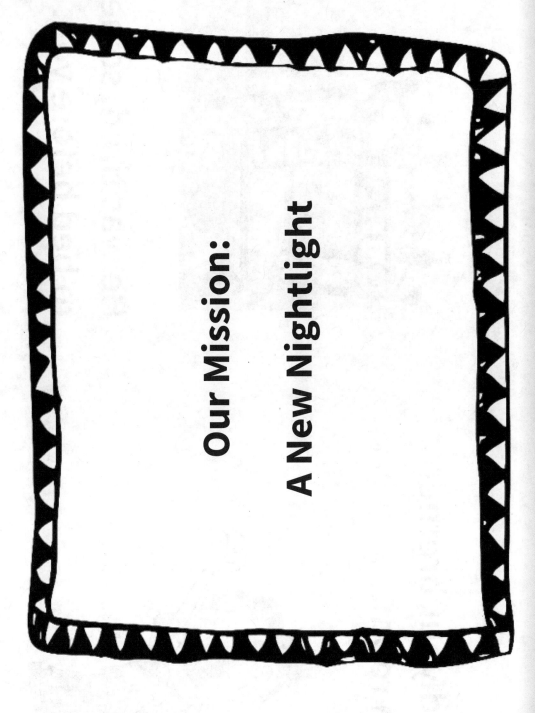

Our Mission:

A New Nightlight

California Instructional Segment

You and your brother
share a room.

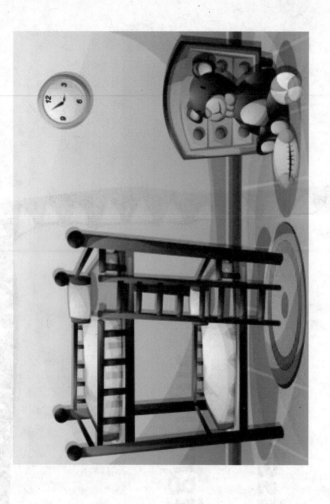

He was tired, so he went
to bed before you.

California Instructional Segment

You quietly walk into the dark room, and—thump!—you hit your toe on your bed frame!

It was too dark for you to see where you were going.

California Instructional Segment

You need a better way to see where you are going in the dark.

You need a night-light!

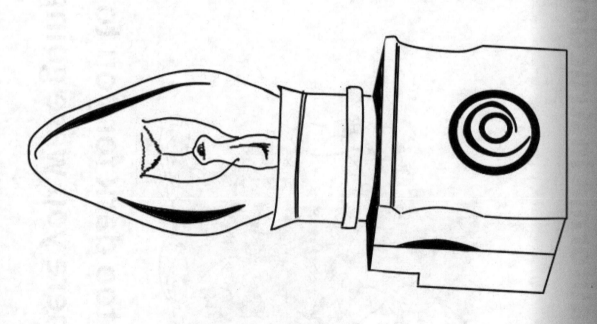

Behavior of Light

Name: _____

Date: _____

Graphic Organizer

★ **This Little Light of Mine** ★

Directions

Draw objects that belong in each of the columns below.

Most Light Passes Through	**Some** Light Passes Through	**No** Light Passes Through

How is light helpful?

🔍 Explore 1

Reflection Fun!

What did you observe on the front side of the mirror?

_____

- -
_____

- -
_____

- -
_____

What did you observe on the back side of the mirror?

_____

- -
_____

- -
_____

Draw what you see when you look at the front of the mirror.

Draw what you see when you look at the back of the mirror.

Name: _____ Date: _____

 **Explore 2**

What Do You See?
Part I: Shine On!

How the Light Behaves	Material
This material lets light pass **all** the way through.	
This material lets **some** of the light pass through.	
This material does **not** let any light pass through.	

Explore 2

Part II: To Be Seen or Not to Be Seen

Group 1: I Saw the Smiley Face on These Objects (reflection).	Group 2: I Did Not See the Smiley Face on These Objects (opaque).

What did you notice about all the materials that you put in Group 1?

_____

_____

What did you notice about all the materials that you put in Group 2?

_____

_____

 **Explore 2**

Part III: Hand Shadow

Draw a picture of what your hand shadow drawing looked like. Make sure you label each hand with Position 1, Position 2, or Position 3.

How was the shadow created?

_____

_____

_____

_____

Why did the size of the shadow change?

_____

_____

_____

_____

Name: _____ Date: _____

Explore 2

What Do You See?

Claim Evidence Reasoning

Thinking like a scientist, write or draw an explanation describing how light acts differently when it hits different things.

When light is blocked by an object, what will it create?

Claim

_____

- -

_____

_____

- -

_____

Evidence Draw an example that proves your claim.

Name: _____ Date: _____

Explore 3

What happens when light hits an object?

Plan it! — Pick two objects.

Test it! — Point the light at the object.

We will use a —

☐ **flashlight.**   ☐ **laser pointer.**

Watch what happens!

Explore 3

Wrap it up! — Draw what you see!

Name: _____ Date: _____

 **Linking Literacy**

Preview and Predict

Preview	Predict
Look at all the pictures.	What do you think the text is about? _____ _____ _____ _____ _____ _____ _____ _____
After making hand puppets and previewing the text, write two things about light you want to learn more about.	I want to learn more about . . . _____ _____ _____ _____ _____ _____ _____ _____ _____ _____

Name: _____ Date: _____

Linking Literacy

Draw and Explain Behaviors of Light

WHILE you read:

Cut out the images at the bottom before reading the STEMscopedia. While you read, listen for the description of each word below, match the picture with the word, and write an explanation of *transparent, translucent, opaque,* and *reflective.* Compare with a partner before gluing.

Word	Picture	Explanation
Transparent		
Translucent		
Opaque		
Reflective		

Linking Literacy

Name: _____ Date: _____

What Will the Light Do?

Draw what will happen to the light when it is shone at each object. Check all the words that could fit in each sentence.

Mineral

Light

The light will _____ when it is shone at the mineral.

☐ reflect ☐ pass through ☐ bounce back ☐ stop

The mineral is: ☐ opaque. ☐ translucent. ☐ transparent. ☐ reflective.

Mirror

Light

The light will _____ when it is shone at the mirror.

☐ reflect ☐ pass through ☐ bounce back ☐ stop

The mirror is: ☐ opaque. ☐ translucent. ☐ transparent. ☐ reflective.

Wood Block

Light

The light will _____ when it is shone at the block.

☐ reflect ☐ pass through ☐ bounce back ☐ stop

The block is: ☐ opaque. ☐ translucent. ☐ transparent. ☐ reflective.

Name: _____ Date: _____

Reading Science

Light

Reading Science
First Grade: Behavior of Light

Light is important in our lives. We need light to see. It is dark when there is no light. We cannot see anything without light.

Some things in nature give off light. The Sun is our biggest light source. Fire and lightning give off light. The Moon reflects light from the Sun.

Some objects also give off light. Lamps, flashlights, and televisions give off light.

Clear things let light pass through. Water and glass let light pass through. Light passes through windows and lights up a room.

Some objects do not let light pass through.
A tree blocks light. A dog blocks light.
A slide on the playground also blocks light.

Some objects let only
some light through.
Some paper lets light
pass through.
So do some curtains
and clothes.

Will light go through you? No! Light will not pass through you. You block the light. When light is pointed at you, it forms a shadow. The shadow is dark. The light cannot reach the part that makes your shadow.

When you point a flashlight at a mirror, the light can be seen on the wall. A mirror can change the direction of the light beam. The mirror reflects the light beam to a different spot in the room.

Light is amazing! It is very important to have light in our lives!

 **Reading Science**

1 Light can pass through all these objects, except–

   A water.

   B paper.

   C trees.

   D curtains.

2 What two things can happen when light shines on something?

   A It can burn and melt it.

   B It can either pass through it or be blocked.

   C A student can see more or less light.

   D It will make its own light or no light.

3 Clear things let light pass through. Objects such as trees, slides, and dogs don't. What can we learn about trees, slides, and dogs from this?

A They are clear.

B They have color.

C They are not clear.

D They let some light pass through.

4 What is "Light" mostly about?

A Light is all around us.

B Light can be seen through water.

C Light can be seen in mirrors.

D If there is no light, it is dark.

Reading Science

5 A student and his friends want to create a shadow-puppet play. In order to make his shadow, the student needs to be sure–

    A the room light is off.

    B the student points a flashlight to his friend's hands.

    C nothing is between the flashlight and his friend's hands.

    D All of the above

📖 Open-Ended-Response

1. You are in a room. All the lights go out. Have the objects disappeared?

_____

_____

_____

What do you need in the room to see clearly?

You need

_____

_____

_____

2. **These materials allow light to pass through:**

_____

_____

_____

_____

These materials do not allow light to pass through:

_____

_____

_____

_____

Open-Ended-Response

3. Draw a picture showing the difference in what you can see in a dark room and what you can see when you turn on the light.

Without light	**With light**

Claim-Evidence-Reasoning

Scenario

Tina's teacher had a cup on his desk. When he placed pens inside, Tina could still see the bottom part of the pens inside the cup, but they looked fuzzy.

Prompt   Why do the bottoms of the pens inside the mug look fuzzy?

Claim: Write a sentence that answers the question.

_____

- -

_____

- -

_____

Evidence: Draw how you know! Label your drawing.

Name: _____ Date: _____

California Instructional Segment

Action Plan

Plan your next birthday party!

- The seasons are spring, summer, fall, and winter.
- You may see the sun and clouds during the day.
- You may see the moon, stars, and clouds at night.

Plan your party.

When is your birthday?

_____

Circle what you think it will be like on your birthday, based on what you know about seasonal patterns.

Season	Number of Daylight Hours	Outside Temperature
Spring	More than nighttime	Hot
Summer	Less than nighttime	Warm
Winter	About the same as nighttime	Cool
Fall		Cold

California Instructional Segment

✏️ **Draw** your party.

Don't forget to include where the party will be and what you will do!

Name: _____

Date: _____

California Instructional Segment

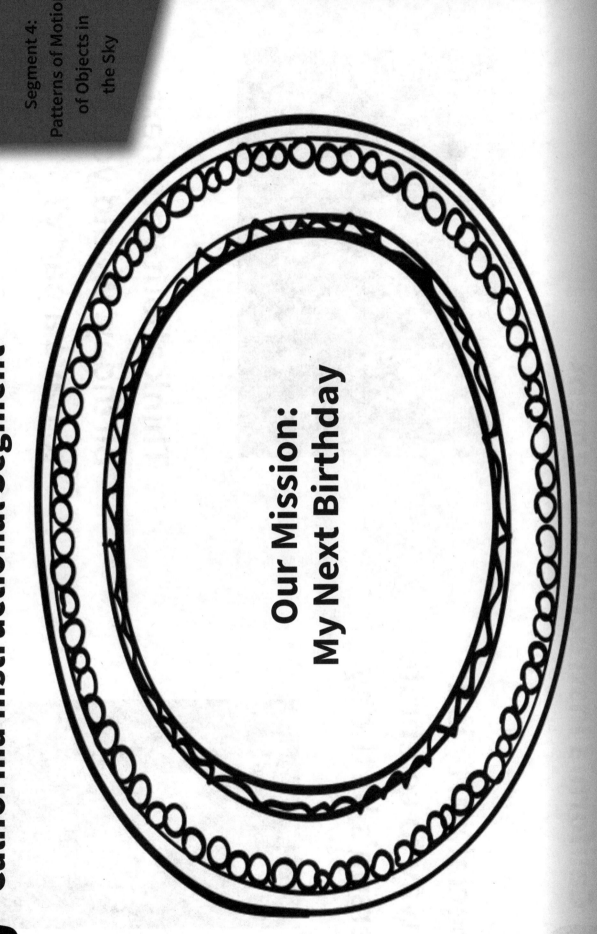

Our Mission: My Next Birthday

California Instructional Segment

A special party is a fun way to celebrate a person's birthday.

Think about your next birthday. Would you like to have a party?

California Instructional Segment

When is your birthday? What season is it in?

Use what you know about seasons to plan your perfect birthday party.

Patterns in Space

Name: _____

Date: _____

Graphic Organizer

 What Do We See

Patterns in Space

What do we see during the day and at night? Add information to the Venn diagram. Draw pictures or write words describing what you learn.

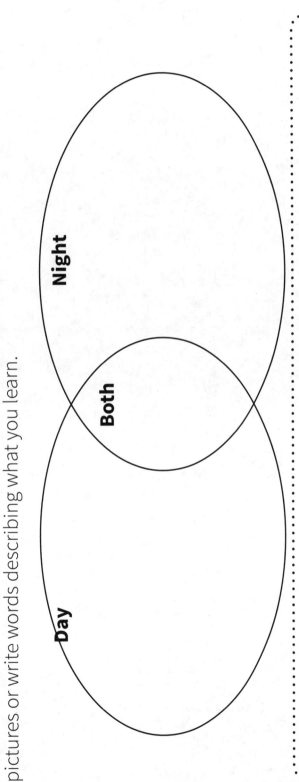

Day

Both

Night

How do things appear to move across the sky?

Name: _____ Date: _____

 **Hook**

Day and Night

1. Watch as your teacher uses a flashlight and a globe to model Earth.
2. What objects do you see in the sky during the day? List them under *Daytime Sky*.
3. What objects do you see in the sky at night? List them under *Nighttime Sky*.

Daytime Sky	Nighttime Sky

4. Do these objects appear to move throughout the day?

_____

_____

_____

Name: _____ Date: _____

 **Explore 1**

Observing Objects in the Sky

Part I: Predictions

Before going outside, you and your partner will predict what you will see in the sky.

Predictions				
	Morning	Noon	Afternoon	Night
Day 1				
Day 2				
Day 3				
Day 4				

Part II: Making Observations

1. Go outside and record everything you see in the sky at that time of day and where that object is in the sky. Remember where you stand to make your observations — it is your special observation post.

2. Repeat these steps every morning, noon, afternoon, and night for 4 days. Make all observations from the same place, your special observation spot.

# Explore 1

Observations				
	Morning	Noon	Afternoon	Night
Day 1				
Day 2				
Day 3				
Day 4				

What patterns did you notice about the sky each morning?

_____

_____

_____

_____

What patterns did you notice about the sky at night?

_____

_____

_____

_____

Name: _____ Date: _____

 # Explore 1

Observing Objects in the Sky
Student CER

How are the objects in the sky different during the day and the night?

Claim

_____

I can see _____ during the day.

I can see _____ and _____ at night

Sometimes I can see the Moon during the _____

Evidence
Draw what you can see in the night sky.

```



```

 Explore 2

Day and Night Patterns

Part I

Choose one sequencing card from the card sort and glue it in the box below.

Draw a picture of what the Sun will look like at the same time tomorrow.

Draw a picture of that the Sun will look like in 2 hours.

Explore 2

Part II

Choose one of the scenario cards and glue it in the box below.

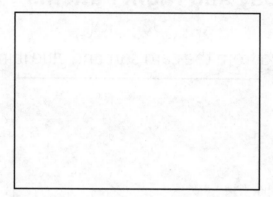

Draw a picture of where the Sun would be during that time.

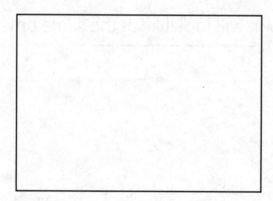

Look at the picture provided. Write your own scenario that would take place when the Sun is in that spot in the sky.

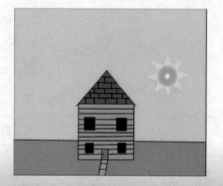

_____

\- - - - - - - - - - - - - - - - - - - -

_____

\- - - - - - - - - - - - - - - - - - - -

_____

Name: _____ Date: _____

 **Explore 2**

The Motion of the Moon and the Sun

Claim Evidence Reasoning

What do we know about the motion of the Sun and the Moon?

Claim   _____   _____

The Moon and the Sun _____ and _____ each day.
                                          _____   _____

We can predict the movement of the Moon and the Sun because they follow a

_____

- -

_____

Evidence

[ ]

Draw how the Moon appears to move through the sky during the night.

[ ]

Name: _____ Date: _____

Linking Literacy

Patterns in Space: True or False

WHILE you read:

Carefully read the statements below. Think about the statement and determine if it is true or false by marking an X in the appropriate box. If the statement is false, rewrite the statement in the correction box to make the statement true.

1.

True	False	Statement:
		The Sun does not light or heat Earth during the day.
Page Number		**Correction:**

2.

True	False	Statement:
		The Sun seems to move across the sky during the day. It rises in the morning and sets at night.
Page Number		**Correction:**

3.

True	False	Statement:
		When we know a pattern, we can use it to predict what will happen next.
Page Number		**Correction:**

Name: _____ Date: _____

 **Linking Literacy**

Draw Your Prediction

AFTER you read:

Think about the patterns we can see of the Sun, the Moon, and stars. Draw the missing part of the pattern by making a prediction of what would happen next.

1. The Sun

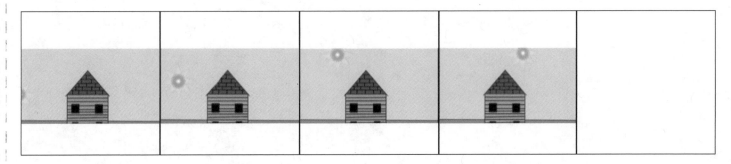

2. The Moon

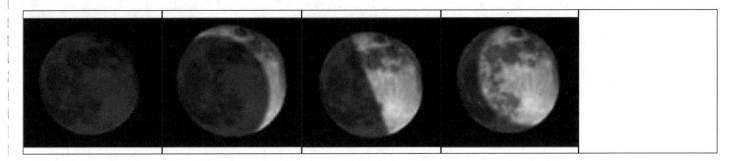

3. Stars

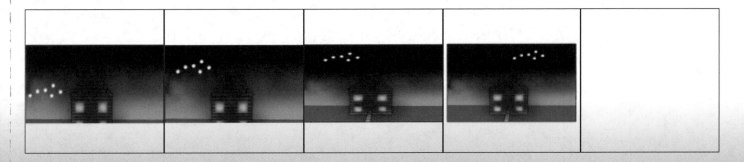

Name: _____ Date: _____

Reading Science

Rabbit's Amazing Day

Reading Science
First: Patterns in Space

Rabbit opened his eyes. It was bright outside. It must have been morning.
Rabbit brushed his teeth. He brushed his fur. It was time to eat breakfast.
Rabbit looked outside. The Sun was shining. It was bright. The Sun was close to a hill. Rabbit put on his hat. He went to his garden.

Reading Science

Rabbit worked in his garden. He pulled carrots. He cut lettuce. It was getting hotter outside. Rabbit dripped with sweat. He looked up. The Sun was above him. The Sun moved! It was not near the hill. "Oh, no!" thought Rabbit.

Rabbit hopped inside. His **burrow** was cool. He made lunch. He had carrots and lettuce. Rabbit felt sleepy. It was time to nap.

Rabbit took a long nap. He looked out the window when he woke up. He saw the Sun by a hill on the opposite side of his burrow. Rabbit was scared. Why was the Sun moving?

Soon, Rabbit did not see the Sun. Where did it go? He saw little dots of light. Rabbit did not know what they were. It was also dark outside. Rabbit called his friend Frog. Frog told him the dots were stars. Rabbit was afraid they would fall on him. Frog told him that they stay in the sky. They would not fall.

Rabbit put on a blanket. It was colder outside now. Rabbit also asked Frog about the other light he saw. It was a dim light. It looked like half of a circle. It was high in the sky. Frog told Rabbit that Earth has one moon.

The Moon goes around Earth once each month. The Moon gives Earth light at night. It also moves across the sky, like the Sun. It moves because Earth spins like a top. It spins once each day. Because it spins, the Sun and the Moon rise and set.

Reading Science

Rabbit felt better. Frog helped him learn about the sky. He stayed outside and looked at the night sky. He did not take his eyes off the sky for a long time. The Moon moved and followed the Sun down over the hill. Much later, the Sun came up. It was morning again! Rabbit was amazed by the sky.

Reading Science

1 Why was Rabbit scared?

A He was alone.

B He had not seen the Sun move before.

C It was getting hot outside.

D He saw the Moon.

2 What is another word for a **burrow?**

A Lunch

B Bed

C Refrigerator

D House

3 What did Rabbit learn from his friend Frog?

A The Sun is hot.

B Earth has two moons.

C He should be scared of the sky.

D He shouldn't be afraid of the sky.

4 Why did it get colder when Rabbit saw the Moon?

A The Moon makes Earth cool.

B The Sun had set.

C The stars make Earth cool.

D The Sun was about to shine.

Reading Science

5 What can the reader tell about the Sun and Moon from the reading?

A The Sun is cold, and the Moon is hot.

B Earth moves the Sun and the Moon.

C The Sun and the Moon can be seen every day.

D The Sun is brighter than the Moon.

Name: _____ Date: _____

Open-Ended-Response

1. Draw your school. Show how the Sun appears to move over your school from morning to night.

Open-Ended-Response

2. At night, we can see the stars in the sky. Can you see the stars during the day?

_____

- -

_____

3. What pattern have you seen the Moon follow?

Draw a pattern you have seen with the Moon.

Name: _____ Date: _____

 # Claim-Evidence-Reasoning

Scenario

Erika recorded what was in the sky during the morning, afternoon, and night for 4 days. Help Erika decide which objects follow a **pattern** and which ones do not.

	Morning		Afternoon		Night		
Day 1	Sun	Clounds	Sun	Clounds	Stars		Moon
Day 2	Sun		Sun		Stars		Moon
Day 3	Sun		Sun		Stars	Clouds	Moon
Day 4	Sun	Clounds	Sun	Clounds	Stars	Clouds	Moon

Prompt

Which object in the sky does not follow the same pattern every day and night?

Claim: _____

Claim: The – – – – – – – – do/does _____

not follow the same pattern every day and night.

Evidence: Write how you know!

_____

_____

_____

_____

_____

Seasonal Patterns

Name: _____

Date: _____

Graphic Organizer

Daylight and Darkness

Each season strip is divided into 24 sections. Each section equals 1 hour. Record the approximate number of daylight and darkness hours during each season by coloring sections yellow for daylight hours and black for darkness hours. Record what activities could be done during each season on each image.

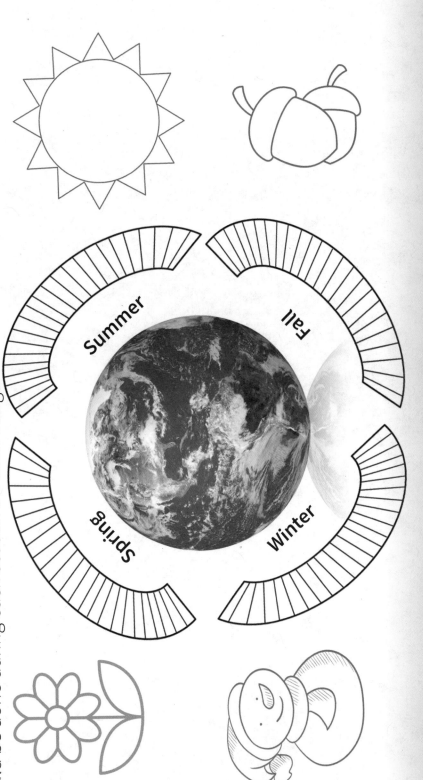

Name: _____ Date: _____

 # Explore 1

Length of Day and Night

Use the graph your class created to fill in the graph below.

Your City _____

Hours of Daylight	Winter (Dec - Feb)	Spring (March - May)	Summer (June - Aug)	Fall (Sept - Nov)
16				
15				
14				
13				
12				
11				
10				
9				
8				
7				
6				
5				
4				
3				
2				
1				

Season

Complete the statements below.

The amount of daylight (changes / does not change) during the year.

We have the **most** daylight during the (winter / spring / summer / fall).

We have the **least** daylight during the (winter / spring / summer / fall).

Name: _____ Date: _____

 **Explore 1**

Length of Day and Night

Claim Evidence Reasoning

In our city, does every day of the year have the same amount of sunlight?

Claim:

We (do / do not) have the same amount of daylight every day.

Evidence:

_____

- -

_____
_____

- -

_____
_____

- -

_____
_____

- -

_____

Name: _____ Date: _____

 **Explore 2**

Fun in the Sun!

Directions

1. Think about activities you can do during the different seasons.
2. Make a rough draft of your poster.
3. Draw or write examples of different activities in each box.
4. Answer the questions on page two.

Winter	Spring
Summer	**Fall**

 **Explore 2**

What activities were you able to do in the summer that you couldn't do in the winter?

_____

- -

_____

- -

_____

How does the amount of daylight affect what you can do?

- -

_____

- -

_____

How does knowing there is more daylight in the summer and less daylight in the winter help you make plans to do activites. .

- -

_____

_____

- -

Name: _____ Date: _____

Linking Literacy

Draw What You Know

Draw what you know about each topic.

Day	Night
Summer	**Winter**

Name: _____ Date: _____

 Linking Literacy

Finish the Sentence

WHILE you read:

Listen to the STEMscopedia about seasonal patterns. Complete the sentences, using the information in the text and the word bank below.

WORD BANK	short	long	day	night
	cold	fall	snow	spring

1. When the Sun shines on your half of Earth, it is _____ .

2. When the Sun is not shining on your half of Earth, it is _____ .

3. It feels _____ in the winter. Some places might have

_____ on the ground.

4. The weather starts to get warmer during the _____ .

5. During the hot summer, the days are _____

and the nights are _____ .

6. Leaves change color as it gets cooler in the _____ .

Linking Literacy

Comparing Day and Night

Compare and contrast day and night.

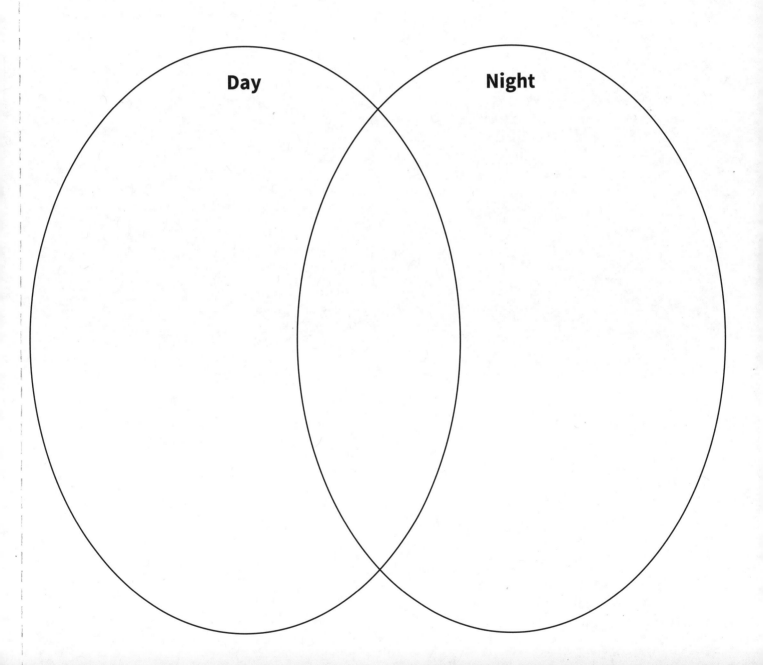

Day

Night

Name: _____ Date: _____

Reading Science

Season After Season

Reading Science
First Grade: Seasonal Patterns

Today is my birthday. I am 6 years old. It's June 23. It's summer, a good time to have a swimming party with my friends and family.

After swimming, we eat cake and ice cream outside on the patio in the shade.

Reading Science

I am glad to have a summer birthday, because the days are longer in the summer. The sunrise is earlier, and the Sun sets later. I can play outside with my friends after dinner.

My sister's birthday is in the fall. It's cooler than in the summer. Fall is a good season to go camping.

We take a hike to see how the leaves are changing. I decide to fall into a pile of them. It's fun to roll around. Try it sometime.

In the fall, the days get a bit shorter. The Sun doesn't come up as early. There is less sunlight, because the sunset is earlier. We build a campfire in the afternoon so we have its light and warmth after dinner.

My dad has a December birthday. It's cold and cloudy outside. We wear coats, because it is winter.

"I want to sit by the fireplace and have hot chocolate and popcorn," Dad laughs. "It's too cold outside."

In the winter, the days are the shortest, and the nights are the longest. We go to school in the dark, and it is already dark at dinnertime.

My mom has her birthday during the next season. Can you guess what season is coming?

Reading Science

Right! It's spring.
"I want to go fishing!"
Mom says.
Wow! What fun! I hope
to catch one.

Most people like spring. The days start to
get longer again. The Sun rises before
we go to school. The Sun sets later,
so we have time to play outside.

We have celebrated four birthdays and four seasons. Almost a whole year has passed. I will be 7 years old once summer comes again.

What is your favorite season?

Can you guess what mine is?

Reading Science

1 Which season has the longest days and the shortest nights?

A Spring
B Summer
C Fall
D Winter

2 What is the name for the time when the Sun comes up?

A Sunday
B Sunlight
C Sunrise
D Sunset

3 Put the seasons in the correct order:

   A Fall, spring, summer, winter
   B Summer, winter, spring, fall
   C Spring, summer, fall, winter
   D Winter, summer, spring, fall

4 Which season has the shortest days and the longest nights?

   A Spring
   B Summer
   C Fall
   D Winter

Reading Science

5 Why did the author use different pictures with each season?

A Because activities and clothing do not change with each season.

B Because activities and clothing do change with each season.

C To make the story more colorful.

D To keep us interested.

Open-Ended-Response

1. What season has the most daylight to play outside?

_____

\- **has the most daylight.**

_____

2. Why is the temperature in summer higher?

The temperature in summer is higher because there is more

_____

\- \-

_____

3. Why is the temperature in winter lower?

The temperature in winter is lower because there is less

_____

\- \-

_____

Open-Ended-Response

4. Use words and a picture to show you playing outside in January.

The season in January is

Name: _____ Date: _____

 # Claim-Evidence-Reasoning

Scenario

Jimmy recorded the amount of **sunlight** during four different days throughout the year. Here is what he recorded.

	Hours of Sunlight Each Day
Day A	9 hours
Day B	11 hours
Day C	13 hours
Day D	15 hours

Prompt

Thinking like a scientist, which of Jimmy's days was most likely in the winter?

Claim:

Day _____ was recorded in the winter.

Evidence: Write how you know!

Winter has the (least / most) amount of sunlight each day.

Write one more piece of evidence from the data.

_____

_____

_____